MALDIVES

PHOTOGRAPHED BY MICHAEL FRIEDEL

TEXT BY MARION FRIEDEL
TRANSLATED BY ANGUS MCGEOCH

EDITION MM

Today the name of The Maldives is on everyone's lips, yet only twenty years ago this republic of coral islands was virtually unknown, remote from the main air and sea routes and forgotten by the world. According to United Nations statistics it was among the 25 poorest countries in the world. But in 1972 a group of Italian divers discovered its underwater paradise of atolls and coral reefs. Tourism in the Maldives was born and has been developing ever since.

In the following year, 1973, Michael Friedel visited the Maldives to take photoghraphs for the German magazine STERN, which published them with the following commentary: "ISLANDS TO DREAM ABOUT....Six months ago a new holiday paradise was discovered in the Indian Ocean: The Maldive Islands. These coral isles are an El Dorado for divers and dreamers. But if you are looking for noise and excitement, stay away."

Michael Friedel was born in 1935 and for nearly forty years he has been taking pictures for leading international magazines including LIFE, PARIS MATCH, GEO and STERN. His photographs of these magically beautiful islands have been seen all over the world. He has travelled extensively, published ten photo-books, and can make himself understood in five languages. He is at home not only in every country under the sun but in all the elements - on land, in the air, on the water and beneath it.

Georg Krose is a pioneer of another kind. Born in 1934, he has a degree in physics and founded a sub-aqua and travel company in Munich, thus making a career out of his twin hobbies. Inspired by Hans Hass and Jacques Cousteau, in 1972 he opened his company's first diving base in Port Sudan on the Red Sea. Always searching for new waters to explore, he was able to confirm what Cousteau had written about the Maldives: that here nature seemed infinite...its dimensions truly vast. He had chanced on a paradise for sun-seekers and scuba-divers, and in 1973 was one of the first travel operators to set up a diving-base there, on the island of Baros. Georg Krose was a founder-member of the International Association of Diving Schools; in this book he describes the difficulties of those early years and gives a brief introduction to diving off the Maldives. Over two decades, Michael Friedel and Georg Krose have observed at first hand the evolution of the tourist industry on the Maldives. Today, tourism is the country's largest source of revenue. On the twentieth anniversary of Maldive tourism, Georg Krose and Michael Friedel were presented with an award by the President of the Maldives.

Marion Friedel, who has written the text, was born in 1945 and has worked as a freelance journalist for the past twenty years. Her travel-writing appears in MERIAN, GEO, STERN and in the books of her husband's photographs. Since 1975 she has been following the changes in the Maldives with very mixed feelings. As in all developing countries, progress brings as many problems as benefits. The pictures in this book capture both the beauty of the islands and the impact of twenty years of headlong development. It is not intended as a travel-guide but as a pictorial document with accompanying information.

Michael Friedel
Marion Friedel
Georg Krose

CONTENTS

Fifteen years ago IHURU, in the North Male Atoll, was a desert island, occasionally visited by fishermen and others who came to gather coconuts. There are hundreds of these Robinson Crusoe isles in the "Paradise of a Thousand Atolls." Of the 1,190 or so islands in the archipelago, only 215 are inhabited. More than seventy of the uninhabited islands have been turned into hotel complexes. Pages 8-9.

From the air, you get a fascinating impression of the Maldive atolls. These islands, which have evolved from circular coral reefs, are known by the Maldivans as "atolu," from which the internationally accepted term "atoll" is derived, to describe any coral island. This, the largest reef formation in the world, is a miracle of nature, yet is created by minute creatures - the coral polyps. Pages 10-11.

In 1978 IHURU was opened up to tourism. The oval islet is just 200 yards wide and can be comfortably walked round in 15 minutes. The number who could stay here used to be limited by the island's fresh water supply. Today, a desalination-plant makes it possible to accommodate up to 74 guests on IHURU. Pages 12-13.

Beneath the water lie the real treasures of the Maldives, and you do not even have to swim in order to get a sight of them. Just put your head below the surface of the crystal-clear water, suffused with sunlight, at the edge of a shallow lagoon, and you will enter a huge, natural aquarium. This is usually enough to addict you for ever to the unique undersea world. Pages 14-15.

In the shade of swaying palm-trees simply let your spirit float free, or immerse yourself in some holiday reading. The uninhabited island of KUDA BANDOS can be reached in a few minutes by boat from the hotel-island of BANDOS. Only on Fridays, the Muslim day of rest, is the island reserved exclusively for the citizens of the Maldive capital, Male. Pages 16-17.

Every day at 6 p.m. the sun bids its brief farewell. Here, close to the equator, the days and nights last an equal 12 hours. Although the temperature only drops by a few degrees at night, it feels pleasantly cool. The relatively high humidity is made tolerable by the gentle but steady sea-breeze. Pages 18-19.

Lonely islands in a wide expanse of ocean. Who does not dream of a paradise scarcely touched by the modern world, where you can live at one with nature in its primordial state? Free from the daily treadmill, no longer governed by the clock, just letting things take their course. Basking in the tranquillity, the space, the warmth, light and colour. Facing text-pages 20 and 22.

If you want to, you can simply shake off all your worries on or under the water. You can swim and snorkel from any of the islands, and most of the resort-hotels are equipped for scuba-diving, sailing and wind-surfing. With a few exceptions, holiday-makers and Maldivans keep to themselves, each on their own islands. Though Muslim, the Maldivan women have always been self-assured and worn no veils. Facing text-pages 24 and 26.

CONTENTS

The population is of mixed Arab, Malay and Singhalese descent. A male foreigner may not approach a Maldivan woman. This kind of inter-racial contact, though it might be a benefit to tourism, is ruled out by the strictly Islamic state. Pages 28-29.

Village life follows a strict pattern, which ensures that everyone lives in harmony. In this world of remote islands, mutual assistance is an essential rule for survival. Daily life takes place chiefly outside, on the broad, neatly swept paths which, on every inhabited island, provide clean, mosquito-free zones. Pages 30-31.

Though the menfolk go off fishing, the women and children scarcely ever leave their island. The islanders are largely self-sufficient. Apart from imported rice, they live mainly on fish and coconut products. This simple and monotonous diet is enlivened, on some islands, by bread-fruit and the fruit of the pandanus, a tree of the palm family. Pages 32-33.

For entertainment in the evening, the big bodu beru drum is brought out and played, exclusively by the men, to accompany their singing and dancing. This drum shows the influence of the African slaves who were shipwrecked on the islands. Today, however, the younger generation prefer rock and disco sounds, as they do all over the world. Pages 34-35.

Once a week, the fishing-boats are pulled up on the beach for repair. They are the islanders' most valuable possessions and essential for their existence. Only those owning boats can hope to make a livelihood. Without boats there would be no fish to eat and no contact with the outside world. Even major repairs are carried out on the islands, without assistance. Pages 36-37.

The great majority of Maldivans still live from fishing in one form or another. It is the main economic occupation of the archipelago. To pursue a shoal of tuna-fish, several boats join together in a fishing-fleet. Yet fishing with nets is unknown in the Maldives; it is all done with hooks and live bait. Pages 38-39.

The sailing freighters which ply between the islands are called *batheli*. They come from the outlying atolls to the capital, Male, which is the only trading and trans-shipment centre. A canopy made of palm-leaves protects the crew and their cargo from rain and spray. Longer voyages can take weeks, even months, when wind conditions are unsettled. Not until the 1970s were the first sailing-ships fitted with diesel engines. Pages 40-41.

MALE, the metropolis and population-centre of the Maldives, is hopelessly overcrowded with houses, over 500 cars and thousands of mopeds, bicycles and boats. The population is officially put at 58,000. It is the only urban settlement in this island state, the nerve-centre of politics, commerce, religion and culture. On an adjacent island, just a few minutes away by boat, lies the airport, the only link with the modern world. Pages 42-43.

CONTENTS

MALE INTERNATIONAL AIRPORT. In 1981, the little landing-strip on the formerly inhabited island of HULULE was, with international aid, extended into a runway for wide-bodied jets. From this static aircraft-carrier, built of coral rock, hotel guests are taken off in water-taxis or by helicopter to the outlying resort islands. Pages 44-45.

Every one of the Maldive islands started life as a little sandbank on a coral reef. Then, by the action of wind, waves, currents and tides, they gradually expanded and evolved into islands. But in the same way as they were created, so may they, as a result of storms or changing tides, disappear once more beneath the sea. Pages 46-47.

A low-lying island is formed. Coconuts are washed ashore, palm-trees grow and their roots stabilize the sand. Sea-birds and hermit-crabs are the first inhabitants. The upper part of the beach and the green interior of the island lie about 6 feet (2 m) above sea-level, while the rest of the visible area, the lagoon, is up to 6 feet under water. Pages 48-49.

All coconut-palms in the Maldives belong to the state and are leased to the islanders. So if you want to take a coconut, you should ask first. The palms of KUDA BANDOS, leaning picturesquely over water, are doomed to disappear, because the protective reef around the island has been damaged. Storms and currents are washing away more and more of the sand. Pages 50-51.

The Maldives are a chain of great and small atolls. RASDU, with a diameter of less than 6 miles (9.5 km) is the smallest of the great atolls. It lies at the northern end of the Ari atoll and comprises four islands. RASDU island itself is inhabited by fishermen, while KURAMATHI and VELIGANDU are tourist resorts. Pages 52-53.

VELIGANDU ISLAND RESORT is a hotel-island in the Rasdu atoll. Its long sandbank is made up of finely ground coral and shells. The rhythm of the tides and the force of the monsoons constantly shift the bank and alter its shape; sometimes it disappears altogether.In the Maldives, the phrase "close to the beach" should always be taken literally.
Pages 54-55.

FARUKOLHUFUSHI, with its large shallow lagoon, ideal for bathing and wind-surfing, is the Club Mediterranée's holiday island. All the islands in the archipelago are the property of the Maldive state. Foreign leaseholders have to invest in their own buildings and facilities, but when the lease expires everything reverts to the Maldive government. Pages 56-57.

EMBUDU Village, in the South Male atoll, has a colourful garden of coral, and a reef which drops away down to 100 feet (30 m) - a happy hunting-ground for snorkellers annd scuba-divers.
Nearby are some exciting places to explore, such as the Vaadhoo channel and a number of sunken ships. This relatively small island has been turned into a 116-bed hotel complex. Pages 58-59.

CONTENTS

If you want nothing more than sun, sea and a little *dolce far niente* - the Maldives offer a veritable paradise. "By Allah, I envy this man, and wish the island belonged to me, so I might retreat entirely from the world." More than six centuries ago, that was the dream of the Moorish traveller, Ibn Battuta. Pages 60-61.

The end of a blazing hot day in the tropics is like balm to the overtaxed senses, a moment for contemplation beneath a pink and gold heaven. For a few minutes, one can gaze over the neighbouring islands to the horizon, until the equatorial night falls like a sudden curtain over the scene. Pages 62-63.

Drinking alcohol is strictly forbidden for the Muslim Maldivans. But they are happy to serve it to hard-currency spenders during the "Happy Hour" on the beach at HALAVELI. Getting rid of the empty drink-cans is a major problem on the islands. Some islands already provide beer on draught, and the Maldivan Coca-Cola and soda-water franchises supply their products in returnable bottles. Pages 64-65.

HALAVELI is a tourist resort situated in the distant Ari atoll. The boat-trip from the airport in a local *dhoni* takes 4-6 hours, and in a speedboat, 2 hours. By helicopter this shrinks to just 20 minutes. It lands on the adjacent, uninhabited island of KANDOLODHU, from where the resort is only a few minutes by boat. Pages 66-67.

There can be no paradise without rain. The weather pattern is mainly determined by the two monsoon seasons, in which the winds blow from opposite directions. Heavy rainstorms occur nainly between May and October. As in most parts of the world, it is impossible to make precise forecasts, but even in the rainy season the sun shines most of the time. Pages 68-69.

Some of the original tourist resorts of the early years were very close to nature, but have now been equipped with fresh-water swimming-pools, cascades, tennis-courts, saunas and jacuzzis. The basic equipment of the rooms includes air-conditioning, satellite TV, bath, fax and telephone. The recently opened LAGUNA BEACH RESORT has been created on the island of Velassaru in the South Male atoll. Pages 70-71.

Dropping anchor off the island of one's dreams. On Cocoa Island, in the South Male atoll, man's ingenuity is in perfect harmony with nature. It is the smallest island hotel in the Maldive archipelago; not measured by the size of the island, but by the number of beds. Cocoa has just eight bungalows, each sleeping 2-3 people. It is possible to rent the whole island for yourself and your friends. Pages 72-73.

People who stay on ELLAIDOO island, on the outer reef of the Ari atoll, are mainly divers. The Munich tour operator, Sub Aqua Tours, has the island under exclusive contract. It has an unusual reef, like an underwater cliff, riddled with little caves. A marvellous, coral-encrusted wreck lies just off the island. Pages 74-75.

CONTENTS

The submarine environment of the Maldives is among the finest that the oceans of the world can offer. Diving here becomes a totally new experience. Since hunting was banned, the only shooting you can do now is with a camera. So the shoals of fish, like the mackerel in this picture, are undisturbed by divers. Pages 76-77.

The diving-instructor Herrwarth Voigtmann has no fear of sharks; since those found in Maldive waters are quite harmless. For many years it was the fashion to lure the sharks with food, and provide the holidaymakers with a spectacular underwater circus. As a result, the creatures lost their natural predatory instincts and begged to be fed. To protect the sharks these shows have now been stopped. Pages 78-79.

Sting-rays are very inquisitive and are not afraid of being touched. Every day as many as five rays swim into the shallow water of the inner reef of IHURU, in order to come into physical contact with Robert, the Swiss diving-instructor, and his pupils. As long as the divers stay relaxed there is no danger from the poisonous sting in the huge fish's tail. Pages 80-81.

The diving and travel expert Georg Krose speaks from 20 years' experience of the development of tourism in the Maldives - of false preconceptions and of expectations far exceeded. But above all he describes the unique diving waters, and how supremely easy it is to learn to dive here. Pages 82-83.

Thanks to a consistent conservation policy, the extraordinary wealth of species in the waters of the Maldives has largely survived the damage caused by hunters and collectors in the early years of tourism, and is now regenerating itself. Just a few of the species can be seen on pages 86-87.

The round, oval, long and crescent-shaped islets never rise more than 6 feet (2 m) above the Indian Ocean. If the sea-level were really to rise significantly in the future, the Maldive archipelago would be totally submerged, and with it the 29 holiday colonies shown on pages 88-89.

For twenty years Michael Friedel and his camera have remained faithful to the Maldives. In 1973 the Sri Lankan Air Force helped him to take the first ever aerial photographs of the Maldive archipelago. For him it was love at first sight; for the Maldivans it was the first time they had seen their islands from the air. The photographer talks about his work and what was made of it. Pages 90-91.

A s I approached by air, there appeared beneath me a strange, almost unreal vision. Islands, a mass of tiny islands in the middle of the Indian Ocean. Out of the dark blue of the sea, more than 6,500 feet (2,000 m) deep, rise the coral reefs. Large and small, round and oval, and the necklace-like atolls. Turquoise lagoons, sandbanks and tiny palm-covered islets, bordered with gleaming white beaches.

From the jetty I look down through crystal-clear water on to vast shoals of multi-coloured fish, such as you would not find in any aquarium. With an escort of flying-fish, a boat brings me to the island of Ihuru.

My feet sink deep in the coral sand. In fifteen minutes I have walked round and explored the litle island. Exciting adventures await only a few yards from my bungalow, on the reef bordering the lagoon. I gaze into a strange and unfamiliar world, an endless natural aquarium. I see shapes that look like stag's antlers, like gigantic brains, ostrich-feathers and fans; I see petrified coral and coral that sways in the water. Through these gardens of glowing coral, fish swim in amazing numbers, of every colour and shape. They do not dart away in fright, nor do they avoid me, so that I can reach out and touch them.

These isles are only the peaks of a sunken land named the Maldives. "Dhivehi Raage" is the name which the inhabitants gave to their island kingdom. And they described themselves as "Dhivehi" - island people. The little isles ranged round circular reefs, they called "atolu," thus giving us the international term "atoll" which is applied to all coral islands.

The Maldive chain of atolls lies 400 nautical miles southwest of the southern tip of India and Sri Lanka (Ceylon). It represents the largest and most impressive reef-formation on earth. Shaped like a necklace, made up of nearly two thousand islands and islets, the atolls extend over a distance of 475 miles (760 km) from north to south, and 75 miles (120 km) from east to west. The Maldive archipelago is a natural barrier thrusting across the sea-route to southern India, and rightly feared by seamen since time immemorial.

Charles Darwin, who first propounded the classical theory of atolls, was lost in wonder: " We are amazed when travellers tell us of the vast pyramids and other great ruins; but even the greatest of these are as nothing when compared with the mountains of stone that have been built up by the activity of innumerable tiny creatures! This is a miracle which, though it may not surprise us when it first meets our eye, does so all the more when we reflect upon it...The infinity of the ocean, the raging of the surf, in sharp contrast to the low elevation of the land and the smoothness of the bright green water within the lagoons, these are things one cannot imagine without having seen them."

There are a number of conflicting theories about the origin of the atolls. Darwin believed they were created when volcanic islands were slowly sinking into the sea. As the land-mass submerged, coral reefs simultaneously grew upwards, forming a ring round the original coastline. Because of its need for light, the coral grew steadily upwards until it was level with the surface of the sea. Since conditions for survival were more favourable on the outer edge, the centre gradually rotted away and became a lagoon. Then storms, waves, tides and currents wash in coral fragments and shells, which fill the lagoon and create a low sandbank. Coconuts float ashore, palm-trees grow and their roots stabilize the beach. Sea-birds, land hermit-crabs and insects are the first visitors to the islands. The archipelago of the Maldives is one of the wonders of the world, created by tiny creatures - the coral polyps.

"When the king of the Maldives claims to rule over 12,000 islands, that is oriental hyperbole. Most of the islands are uninhabited and contain nothing but trees. Others are mere heaps of sand, which are covered by water when the tide is particularly high..." Thus spoke the German philosopher Immanuel Kant, who admittedly never once left his native Königsberg, but took issue with this exaggeration in his "Lectures on Natural History."

Today, the Maldivans make more modest claims. They talk of twenty-six natural atolls, which are grouped into nineteen administrative atolls; and of 1,190 islands, of which 215 are inhabited. The entire land surface of this maritime nation totals only 115 square miles (298

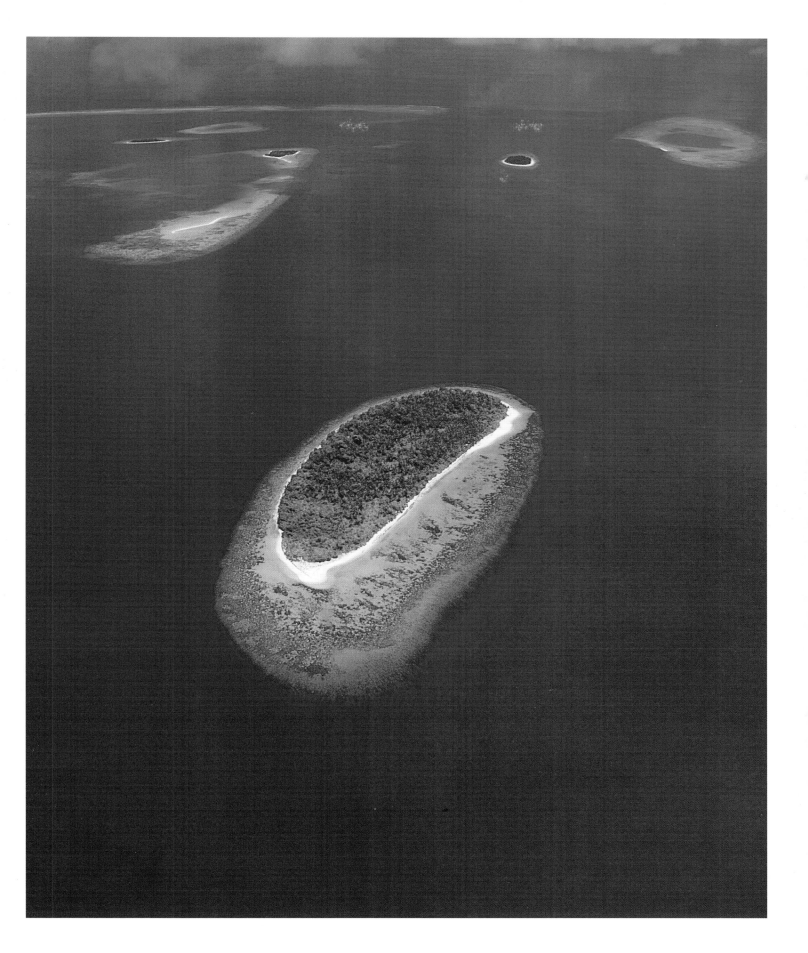

sq.km), which is equivalent to a medium sized city.

The size and number of islands in this coral republic are not immutable figures. Coral reefs are extremely sensitive and slow-growing organisms. They can take as much as a century to grow one meter. Slight shifts in the balance of nature are enough to make whole islands sink beneath the sea, while other new ones are being born.

The early history of their settlement is obscure. According to one myth, Singhalese women were the first to set foot on the islands. They called their realm "Mahiladipa" - the islands of women. From this name it is not difficult to derive the "Maldives" of today. Erotic legends were woven around these women; they took explorers, merchants and shipwrecked sailors as their lovers and bore them children. The men were mainly Arabs, but also Africans and Malays. Their features can be seen today in the faces of the population. Tales of these islands of paradise are centuries old. The first description of the Maldives was written by the Moroccan explorer and adventurer, Ibn Battuta, who visited the "Sultan's Islands" in the 14th century, and stayed there for more than a year: "From the fruit of the palm the people make milk and honey. From this food, and from their fish, the inhabitants gain remarkable endurance in the practice of love-making. The achievements of the islanders in this respect are astonishing...When a ship arrives the crew gets "married." When the sailors leave again, they abandon their women, so the marriages are but brief ones." Battuta went on to report that even in the 12th century the islands were a well-organized state.

In the year 1135 the Buddhist Sultan and his court were converted to Islam by a devout Moslem from North Africa named Abu-ul-Barat. With this event begins the officially recorded history of the Maldives. Together with Qatar and Oman, the Maldive republic is today one of the only three countries in the world which are 100 per cent Muslim. The ruling class profited in a number of ways from the islamicisation of the archipelago. The islands became part of the Arab trading network, so that rare and valuable goods came in from abroad. The strict Islamic code of law made government easier and strengthened the role of the central authority over the widely scattered island kingdom.

In this period, the Maldivans literally grew for themselves the coinage of international trade, just as in the Land of Cockaigne. They laid branches down in the lagoons, on which grew thousands of cowrie-shells, which were a very important currency throughout Africa, India, Arabia and Asia. Since the end of the slave-trade, the cowrie, or monetaria moneta, to give it its scientific name, has played no part in world trade. Throughout the centuries, by virtue of their geography, the Maldives remained independent. They were never of interest to colonizers, since apart from fish and copra, there was nothing to be had there.

The Portuguese only stayed there from 1558 to 1575 and were driven back by the Maldivans to their Indian base in Goa. Three hundred years later, the British declared the Maldives a protectorate, but never became involved in the internal affairs of the sultanate.In 1965 the Maldives gained their political and economic independence.

In the 1950s, Hans Hass discovered the fascinating world of the Maldive atolls and coral reefs on his expedition in "Xarifa."

In his wake came diving enthusiasts, who formed the vanguard of the tourist invasion. In 1972 a turbo-prop aircraft of Air Lanka would leave Colombo and after a good two hours flight, would land at the airstrip on Hulule island.

Four policemen controlled the traffic on this island in spite of its having no cars. Their only job was, once or twice a day, to check the four paths which crossed the airstrip, and see that no villagers or goats wandered in front of the aircraft.

Visitors sailed out to the islands of Kurumba or Bandos in dhonis, the Maldivan fishing-boats. These were the first uninhabited islands to have simple bungalows erected on the beach. To do this, literally everything had to be imported: every nail, screw and water-tap, every piece of corrugated iron, every wash-basin, every bowl, the canned beer, the wine, even the writing-paper for the holiday-makers from Europe.

Shrewd scouts and pioneers of the travel industry marketed the little islands, with their waving palms, white

beaches and blue lagoons, as "dream islands." With their yearning for faraway places and desire to see these fabled islands, more and more sun-worshippers, snorkellers and divers arrived from all over the world.

At first, the sleepy coral republic did not know what to make of this invasion. Having lived for centuries from little else but coconuts and fishing, cut off from the outside world, they were propelled, overnight, into the demanding, hi-tech culture of 20th century mass tourism.

Being alert and intellegent, they quickly realized that they could earn foreign currency from the things they had in abundance: sea, sun, coral reefs and islands. Today the nation's cash-registers are filled with US dollars. Having been an independent Islamic republic since 1965, the government made tourism a Maldivan business right from the start and holds the reins firmly in its hands. All the islands are owned by the state and are not for sale. Foreign investors in the hotel sector are only accepted for a limited period. When a lease expires, the buildings and other facilities revert to Maldive ownership. This ambitious young nation intends to remain master in its own land, and tries, as far as possible, to manage all the aspects of tourism itself. One soon appreciates the Maldivans as tolerant and open-minded people, who learn quickly from new experience and, when necessary, draw the right conclusions from it.

n only ten years the Maldivans had made the leap into the 20th century. In 1972 the first hotel was opened, in 1977 the first jets landed and satellite telephones were installed, in 1978 colour television...- Between 1976 and 1981, as tourist traffic was building up, the island of Hulule was evacuated and levelled with coral stone to provide a runway for jumbo jets. It became an air crossroads in the Indian Ocean. The atolls of the Maldives, which from the air look like floating dreams, became, in 1981, a charter-flight paradise, only 10 hours by air from Europe. At first the globe-trotting Germans were in the majority, but they were followed by Italians, British, Japanese, Swiss, Scandinavians, Australians, and even a few dedicated divers from the United States.

The term "tourist resort" is hardly adequate. Refuge, or "de- stressing centre", better describes any of the 70 or more islands on which hotels have been built, predominantly in the bungalow style. That is to say: a reception lobby, a restaurant, a bar, guest bungalows, and nearly always a diving and windsurfing school. The size of a resort is not measured by the dimensions of the island, which can usually be walked round in twenty minutes or less, but by the number of beds it has. In the last few years the introduction of sea-water desalination plants has removed the bottleneck caused by the lack of natural fresh water, and made possible a considerable increase in accommodation. Paradise is getting a little crowded.

Many of the resorts were once simple and close to nature, but have since been drastically modernised. The first visitors were the sort of people who appreciated not having to wear shoes or elegant clothes. They were pioneers who enjoyed making do with the elementary facilities of the islands.

But organised tourism set its own norms and demanded a guaranteed standard. The Maldivans take great pride in their first international five-star resorts, built with their own resources, such as Kurumba and Laguna Beach.

With a few exceptions the visitors and the indigenous population keep to their own separate islands. Resort guests usually only get to know the locals as male hotel staff or boatmen. In Ibn Battuta's day, friendly contact between the races was common, and he wrote enthusiastically of the "delightful company offered by the womenfolk." In today's Islamic regime, however, any such contact is considered undesirable, and would be harshly punished - even though it might be beneficial for tourism. The unusually high divorce rate here - according to UNESCO, the highest in the world - is something the Maldivans must sort out for themselves.

This strictly regulated picture-book paradise is divided into three regions, and three corresponding strata. Firstly there are the holiday islands, principally in the North and South Male atolls and the Ari atoll; then there is the only city, Male, on the island of the same name, which for centuries has been the economic and cultural hub of the Maldives. Finally, there is the rest of the archipelago. Neither the western lifestyle of the holidaymakers in their

hard-currency enclaves, nor the high standard of living of the old-established citizens of Male, wielding an oriental form of power though traditonal family networks, have anything in common with life in the rest of the archipelago. Here the majority of the population lives, spread over nineteen lonely and far-flung atolls. Life in these self-sufficient village communities is peaceful, though monotonous and stricly ordered. The men are predominantly fishermen, who garner with much effort and little profit the republic's principal export and the main source of food for its people. The all-purpose means of transport is the dhoni, a smaller version of the Arab dhow. They are built in a traditional manner, from timber of the coconut palm, without using nails. Because of the long distances within Maldivan waters, contact with outlying islands, let alone with the rest of the world, is minimal. Voyages can last weeks or even months, and the tricky navigation through reefs and lagoons makes every trip an alarming adventure.

Centuries before the fictional hero Robinson Crusoe appeared on the literary scene, the real-life explorer Ibn Battuta declared his wish to be banished to paradise on one of the many isles of the Maldive archipelago: "We sailed to a very small island, on which stood but one house. In it dwelt a weaver with his wife and children. He had a boat in which he went out fishing or sailed to one of the neighbouring islands. Banana-plants and coconut palms provided food for the taking. By Allah, I envy this man, and wish the island belonged to me, so that I might retreat from the world and await my final hour."

"Back to nature, preferably on a desert island." At the beginning of the 1980s the German travel company, Sub Aqua Tours, made this dream come true. "Be another Robinson Crusoe - alone on your own island; we arrange your trip with nothing included." All that was offered was the flight, and a boat to take you to an uninhabited isle. Equipped with basic provisions, a US Navy survival manual and a fishing-line, the over-civilized seeker of paradise could spend up to three weeks rediscovering his natural roots. A marvellous idea in theory, it failed in practice due to a surfeit of nature and solitude, which brought on a mild form of dementia, and because kindly native fishermen would try to rescue the lonely exiles. For, even today, the severest punishment for any Maldivan is to be banished to a strange island. So the Crusoe-island holidays were permanently dropped from the tour-operator's catalogue.

Instead, there is a modern variant in the form of day-excursions in a large helicopter, for a "Robinson Crusoe picnic" in the Ari atoll. Accompanied by a tour-leader, 25 would-be Crusoes share a beach buffet for two hours on an uninhabited island.

For me, the loveliest way to travel around the Maldive atolls is in a safari-boat. These are dhonis, which are fitted out, with modest comforts, for fairly long voyages. As you glide through the archipelago and then out into the infinite expanse of ocean, you suddenly see another island on the horizon, and it seems that you have reached the goal of all your dreams.

Miniature islands, like the Maldive atolls, have always aroused a romantic yearning for untroubled bliss, for a charmed existence, free from the anxieties of civilization. Away from the hectic, depersonalizing routine of making a living, one dreams of never again being a slave to mere economic necessity.

Marion Friedel

t was 1972, and I was enquiring from Swissair about connections to the Maldives. The desk-clerk was baffled. "The Maldives? Where are they?" he asked. He was by no means the first person to display total ignorance of their whereabouts. The only possibility was to take a scheduled flight to Colombo, and on from there in a small propellor aircraft of the Sri Lankan Air Force, which finally landed us on the Maldive island of Hulule. In the 1950s, one of Hans Hass' companions on his "Xarifa" expedition was I.Eibl-Eibesfeldt, whose book "In the Kingdom of a Thousand Atolls," had filled me with great curiosity.

With tremendous anticipation at being one of the first people ever to dive on these fabled coral reefs, I set foot on Maldive soil.

Then as now, the local fishing-boats,or dhonis, provided the main means of transport between the islands. When forced below deck by bad weather, we had to compete with hundredweight sacks of rice, free-rolling coconuts and soggy cartons of beer. The journey from Europe to one's chosen Maldive island could take a wearying 36 hours. The beauty of the island landscape was not, in those days, accompanied by the comforts of civilization. Accommodation was in simple huts woven from palm-leaves. For lack of anything else, our daily diet was fish à la Maldives: fish with rice, rice with fish, and of course coconut. What a contrast there was between the rather featureless surface of the islands, and the infinite variety of the underwater world.

There are no superlatives adequate to describe what one saw beneath the surface of the sea. There can be nowhere in the world where the "local" reef, just a few yards from your bed, is so teeming with life: tropical fish of every colour and shape, so tame that they eat out of your hand. Shoals of surgeon-fish, colourful parrot-fish, perch, moray-eels, shrimps, rays, and now and then an inquisitive shark - a limitless aquarium. This world is easily accessible to anyone who can use a snorkel, mask and inflatable raft. The miracle begins in the warm, shallow waters of the lagoon.

In 1973 I opened the first diving-base on the island of Baros in the North Male atoll. To do this, more than two tons of diving equipment had to be laboriously flown in, requiring several flights, then shipped across to Baros in dhonis. From the outset I realized that, in the long run, only rigorous protection could keep this submarine universe in something like its primordial state. Anyone who has dived in the Mediterranean, knows what damage has been caused by underwater hunting and the unrestricted collecting of shells and coral. Anything left has been wiped out by dynamite fishing. The Mediterranean is practically dead. To come across any fish there at all is quite an event. Even in the Maldives, the reefs were practically hunted bare in the space of year. Everything that came too close to the divers' spears fell victim to hunting-fever, and the sensitive ecological balance of the atolls was on the brink of destruction. Even so, it was no easy matter convincing the Maldivan government of the need for careful conservation of the undersea world. The islanders had never touched their reefs and only went after deep-water fish. Today, a strict ban on underwater hunting is enforced. You may only shoot with a camera, and all you are allowed to gather is impressions. All the diving bases work tirelessly with the government to see that these rules are obeyed.

he picture-book islands of the Maldives create the perfect illusion of a south-sea paradise. One is carried away with thoughts of living close to nature, in romantic solitude under the palms. But twenty years of tourism in the Maldives have proved to me that a "real" desert island would be too much for most present-day travellers.

Before your trip, find out exactly what the different islands have to offer, for example: size, number of beds, facilities, what sports are catered for and what entertainment is provided. Think carefully about what you are prepared to do without, and what you have always wanted to try. Among the seventy-two tourist resorts, everybody can find at least one to suit their taste, and several offer the luxury of Florida or Acapulco. But above all you should consider whether you are fit for "island duty", because sooner or later everyone who takes a holiday in the Maldives gets stricken, at least once, by island madness.

The physical limitations of the little islands, which can quickly be walked round and explored, throw the visitor back on his own resources. After, at most, a few days of unaccustomed peace, the holidaymaker begins to pine for his normal stressful life, he is plunged into an abyss of boredom, the island becomes a prison with three meals a day. These tiny isles can put you to the test in many ways. You soon find things to complain about. Either you have brought the wrong person with you, or there are ants in the bed, or a cockroach in the bath, the water in the shower is a bit salty, the generator is too noisy, the air-conditioning is faulty, the beer is warm, the food monotonous, and then when it starts raining as well...

If life on land is less than perfect, underwater it is extremely attractive, which is why 90 per cent of Maldive holidaymakers spend most of their time down there. Some begin rather tentatively, by hiring a mask and snorkel and exploring the magnificent coral gardens around their resort island. Others, and they are the majority, are already hooked and come here just for the diving. It is only a short step from one's first gasps through a snorkel to total diving addiction.

Once your interest is aroused, you will progress by taking diving lessons. They say that God invented diving in the Maldives. These are certainly the most perfect waters for diving - bar none. Only a stone's throw from your bungalow you can be diving in waters of almost undescribable beauty. Learning to dive here is child's play. The water is clear and pleasantly warm, the coral positively glows, and the variety of fish is incomparable. Where in the world would you find more beauty beneath the sea?

With your first steps into the waters of the lagoon you can gaze on these miracles, get accustomed to your equipment and enjoy the feeling of weightlessness.

In parallel with the actual "wet" diving instruction, there are classes in the theoretical aspects. Professionally qualified diving-instructors will train you according to internationally established guidelines. This means that, after completing the course, the pupil can be sure of receiving a recognized diving certificate, which will enable him or her later to dive anywhere in the world. The courses are designed to have plenty of variety. After each theoretical lesson there is a little quiz, to make sure that you have hoisted in all the "dry" stuff.

On the theoretical side, the pupils learn the basic physics of diving, absorb a great deal about the sea and the creatures in it, and are instructed in diving safety and how to plan a diving expedition. In the practical exercises, they learn how to handle diving-gear safely, and how to communicate with their diving-partner under water. After the last theoretical lesson they have to pass a graduation test. In the shallow lagoon they take their first underwater gulps of air. Even on their first real dive, on the reef nearest their resort island, the trainee divers can enjoy the beauty of the undersea world and the feeling of weightlessness. But what makes a good diver is the experience gained from many dives, in which safety and enjoyment go hand in hand. That is why they return again and again to this divers' paradise.

Georg Krose

FISH AND MARINE LIFE

Emperor Anglefish

Sea Star

Trunkfish

Soldierfish

Gray Reef Shark

Mackerel

Anglefish

Threeband Humbug

Racoon Butterflyfish

Blue Surgeonfish

Manta Ray

Nurse Shark

Sharpnose Puffer

Surgeonfish

Yellowfin Fusilier

Squirrelfish + Rock Cod

Maldive Clownfish

Seaturtle

Scorpionfish

Giant Triggerfish

Moray + Grouper

Moray

Oriental Sweetlips

Firefish

Grouper

Collared Butterfish

Threespot Damselfish

Whitespottet Puffer

Blue Face Anglefish

Ihuru

Thulhagiri

Bandos

Club Med - Farukolhufushi

Nakatchafushi

Kurumba

Vabbinfaru

Baros

Embudhu Finolhu

Kanifinolhu

Biyadoo

Dhigufnolhu

Kandooma

Furana

Cocoa

Embudhu

Laguna Beach

Vaadhu

Villivaru

Kuramathi

Veligandu

Ellaidoo

Halaveli

Nika Hotel

Fesdu

Bathala

Mayaafushi

Ari Beach

Kuredu

The sailing-dhoni "ALADIN" was the first native boat to be fitted with an engine, in 1974, and it remains to this day my favourite means of travel. Thanks to its shallow draught of only 2 ft. 6 ins. (80 cm), I can get through any reef and into the shallow lagoons of the tree-covered and inhabited islands. Without the help and valuable advice of Ahmed Adam, the builder and owner of the "ALADIN" I would not have been able to take many of my photos. His experienced crew are the true pathfinders through this labyrinth of reefs. There are very few skippers in the Maldives who know the reefs beyond their home atoll and who dare make such trips as ours. The week-long voyages aboard the "ALADIN" brought me and my wife to islands whose inhabitants had never seen Europeans before. At first the women and children hid themselves, only to emerge a short while later, driven by curiosity and dressed in their best clothes, to pose for the camera. We spent most nights sleeping in hammocks on uninhabited islands, to the horror of the crew. They stayed on board in fear of the island's spirits.

We came upon virgin waters, where the fish had never seen a diver before. Spiny perch and reef-sharks swam within an arms-length of us, to defend their territory. My first attempts at diving, with over 50 kilos of equipment and no buoyancy-control jacket, nearly proved fatal. I must have seen 200 sharks before finally getting one in my viewfinder. With the help of a colleague, Herrwarth Voigtmann, who now teaches diving on Maayafushi, I took my first close-ups of sharks. Because of the strong current, I had tied myself to some coral with a nylon line. As many as seven sharks then decided to take an interest in us. They even swam right between my legs without touching me. I managed to get a shot from just a foot (30 cm) away.

My aerial photos of the islands caused a sensation among the Maldivans. They had never seen their home so clearly from above.

When first published, my pictures established a new image of the Maldives. For the Maldivans it was a completely new experience to see their islands through the eyes of a foreigner. The romanticised vision of the tourist was something that, until then, had never entered their mind. Nowadays I come across my images in endless variations, on batiks, posters and T-shirts.

On the 10th anniversary of the republic's independence a series of postage-stamps was issued, featuring four of my photographs, and at the same time my first post-cards, posters and stickers appeared.

To capture the phenomenon of the Maldives, I had to photograph them from the air, from sea-level and underwater. That is why I learned to dive in the Maldives twenty years ago.

For this work in three dimensions I currently use a MINOLTA 9xi with or without an underwater casing.

When travelling I use five to seven different cameras and ten lenses ranging from 16mm to 500mm. For aerial photography all this equipment is put to use. As a protection against spray and in water up to 15 feet (5 m) deep I put the MINOLTAS in light, flexible casings made by EWA MARINE. I shoot exclusively on KODAKCHROME 25, 64 and 200 ASA film. To protect them from heat and fading in the tropical climate, I carry cameras and film around in small refrigerated bags. I only use a polarizing filter when shooting from the air, so as to bring out more clearly the sandbanks and reefs which lie just below the surface. Most of my aerial shots are taken at noon, with the sun directly overhead and, if possible, at low tide. Then the radiant colours of the different depths of water, and of the gleaming white beaches, can be seen in all their beauty.

The Maldives lie on the equator, so the light is harsh and the contrasts are great. Choosing the right exposure is a hell of a problem. An exposure-meter won't help. You just have to rely on experience. The best times for taking pictures are between 6 and 8 o'clock in the morning, and after 4 o'clock in the afternoon. The weather I dream of, for taking photographs in the Maldives, is when the air is clear after rain, the sun is shining and there is no wind. Then the blue of the sky and the blue of the sea blend into one, and the little clouds are reflected on the water between the islands.

In 1973, I had to make several sorties in order to capture the Maldives from the air. In exchange for US dollars the Sri Lankan Air Force were extremely helpful. The distance of over 500 miles, the lack of radio communication and an only partially tarmac'd airstrip, combined to make the undertaking quite an adventure. The four-engined military aircraft was too heavy and too fast, and I had to return to Colombo without any pictures. For the second flight the pilot risked flying a four-seater Cessna by the seat of his pants, with only a compass for guidance. After three and a half hours, to my great relief, we sighted the first of the Maldive reefs. An hour later we reached the island of Hulule. In the twenty years since then, I have clocked up several hundred flying-hours. Getting airborne becomes easier all the time. The HUMMINGBIRD helicopter service today offers daily photographic flights round the archipelago.

FACTS ABOUT THE MALDIVES

GETTING THERE

From Europe there are fast, direct charter flights with: LTU, CONDOR, BALAIR, LAUDA AIR, AIR EUROPE, ALITALIA, AUSTRIAN AIRWAYS, STERLING AIRWAYS,TRANSWEDE AIRWAYS and UNIFLY EXPRESS. Scheduled flights are more expensive and take longer: AIR LANKA, EMIRATES AIRWAYS, AIR INDIA, PAKISTAN INTERNATIONAL AIRWAYS, SINGAPORE AIRLINES.

ARRIVAL AND CUSTOMS

Citizens of EC countries and of the USA require no visa but must have a passport valid for at least three months. It is forbidden to import: alcohol, pork meat products, dogs and pornography.

HOTELS

It is essential to book into an island resort before you leave home. Anyone who travels independently and tries to book in on arrival, pays top prices.

BOATS AND TAXIS

The all-purpose form of transport is the native dhoni, converted for use as a passenger ferry. They take you from the airport to the island resort. To reach the more distant atolls you can book a helicopter service. Cars can only be hired on the main island, Male.

TRAVEL SEASONS AND RAINY SEASONS

Changes in the weather are mainly brought about by the monsoons. The south-west monsoon lasts roughly from the end of April until September. Towards the end you get rain, high winds and thunder-storms. The period of the north-east monsoon, from December until April, is the driest season. All year round, the average temperature remains around 30 deg. C., and the temperature of the water in the lagoons is between 27 and 29 deg.C.

CLOTHING AND EQUIPMENT

The prevailing atmosphere on most of the holiday islands is relaxed and informal. Ladies can leave their jewelry and high-heeled shoes at home. But you should bring plenty of easy-care cotton clothes, because laundries and dry-cleaners are rare. Do not forget to bring sun-cream with a high protection factor, after-sun lotion, mosquito-repellant, sun-hat, bathing costumes, sandals and a track-suit, as well as plenty of reading-matter and a well-fitting diving-mask.

MEDICINE

In addition to any medication you take regularly, bring analgesics and anti-diarrhoea tablets, sticking-plaster, antiseptic ointment for small wounds caused by coral, and a lotion for sunburn. The only medical care available is at a basic hospital in Male and from a private service.

CURRENCY

The national currency is the Maldive Rufiyaa. US dollars, preferably in the form of travellers-checks, are the safest method of payment. With other currencies you lose a lot on exchange. The major credit-cards are generally accepted.

ELECTRICITY

The current on all the islands is 220 volts.

TIME

Depending on the season The Maldives are 4-5 hours ahead of Britain and 3-4 hours ahead of continental Europe.

TELEPHONE AND TELEVISION

From most of the islands you can telephone or send faxes to the rest of the world via satellite without difficulty. Maldive Television broadcasts news in English, and on some islands it is possible to receive satellite TV.

RELIGION AND ETIQUETTE

Friday is the Maldivans' holy day. Nude bathing is forbidden on all the islands. On expeditions to Male and the other inhabited islands the prescribed dress code should be observed. The shoulders and upper arms should be covered, and shorts are severely frowned upon.

SPORT AND LEISURE

You can borrow board-games from the hotels, and table-tennis and volley-ball competitions between guests and staff are arranged every evening. On some islands there is a weekly disco or a live band. Night fishing followed by a barbecue is organized by most of the resorts. Some have tennis, sailing and fitness programmes. Almost all the islands provide instruction in diving and windsurfing. Equipment can be hired. One-week diving-safaris to the most beautiful spots, are organized by Sub Aqua Reisen.

CLIMATIC TABLES

	Jan.	Feb.	Mar.	Apr.	May	Jun.	Jul.	Aug.	Sep.	Oct.	Nov.	Dec.
Mean maximum daytime temperature (deg. C.)	31	31	32	33	33	32	32	32	32	32	31	31
Mean minimum night-time temperature (deg. C.)	24	24	25	26	26	25	25	25	25	24	24	23
Mean daily hours of sunshine	7	8	7	6	5	5	6	6	6	6	6	6
Mean monthly days with rain	11	2	6	9	17	15	11	12	12	19	12	17

EXPEDITIONS

A day-trip in a dhoni to other resort islands and to Male, is often the only chance you will have of leaving your own island and seeing something of the country and its people. In Male you will have an opportunity to observe the life of the indigenous population at closer quarters. The newly built mosque and the small museum are worth seeing. There are 15-minute helicopter flights around the Male atoll, organized by Hummingbird. A one-week safari in a basic dhoni, which can sail over the reefs and into shallow lagoons, is one of the absolute high points of any holiday in the Maldives. It is the best way of getting to know the islands and their underwater world.

BOOKS OF TRAVEL AND DISCOVERY

ANDERSON, Charles, "Living Reefs of the Maldives," Male
COUSTEAU, Jacques-Yves, "The Ocean World", Abrams Pub., New York 1985
DARWIN, Charles, "Structure and Distribution of Coral Reefs," 1984 edition, University of Arizona Press, USA.
FRIEL, Bob, "Underwater Maldives", Male 1989
HUXLEY, Anthony, "Encyclopedia of the World's Oceans and Islands," London 1969
MINER, Roy Waldo, "Coral Castle Builders of Tropic Seas," National Geographic Society Magazine, Washington, June 1934
BATTUTA, Ibn, "Travels in Asia and Africa 1325-54," 1983 edition, Darf Pub., London
DARWIN, Charles, "Voyage of Charles Darwin," Edited by C. Ralling, BBC Pubs., London 1978
PYRARD, F. "Voyage of Francois Pyrard de Laval," published by the Hakyut Society, c/o The British Library, London

SHOPPING AND SOUVENIRS

It is scarcely worth buying duty-free goods in Male. In the shops you can buy T-shirts, scarves, postcards, posters, stickers, painted wooden boxes, coral jewelry and sharks' teeth. It is perfectly acceptable to haggle over the price. You will also be offered things made from tortoise-shell and sea-shells, which come from protected species. If you are caught with these at the airport, they will be confiscated and you will have to pay a fine of US$500 on the spot.

EATING AND DRINKING

All the island resorts serve international cuisine. Most of them have only one restaurant with no choice of menu. A very few have a coffee-shop and a restaurant with an à la carte menu. Alcoholic drinks are available on all the holiday islands. In Male there are several small restaurants, but they are not allowed to serve alcohol.

MAP OF THE MALDIVES

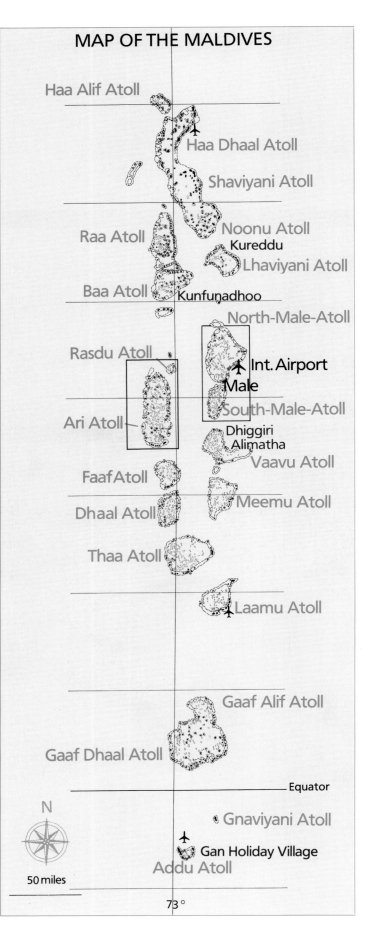

Haa Alif Atoll

Haa Dhaal Atoll

Shaviyani Atoll

Raa Atoll

Noonu Atoll

Kureddu

Lhaviyani Atoll

Baa Atoll

Kunfunadhoo

North-Male-Atoll

Rasdu Atoll

Int. Airport
Male

Ari Atoll

South-Male-Atoll

Dhiggiri
Alimatha

Vaavu Atoll

Faaf Atoll

Dhaal Atoll

Meemu Atoll

Thaa Atoll

Laamu Atoll

Gaaf Alif Atoll

Gaaf Dhaal Atoll

Equator

N

Gnaviyani Atoll

Gan Holiday Village

Addu Atoll

50 miles

73°

REPUBLIC OF MALEDIVES

The islands, grouped into atolls, stretch along the 73rd meridian between latitudes 0 42' south and 8 10' north, for a distance of 468,3 miles (753,6 km), with a width of 73,4 miles (118,1 km) from east to west.
The shortest distance from the mainland of India is 217 miles (350 km) and from Sri Lanka 460 miles (740 km).
Geography: exclusively coral island atolls.
Size: 1,190 islands with a land area of 115 square miles (298 sq.km).
Sea area: approx. 41,500 square miles (107,500 sq.km)
Total population: 214,139 (1990)
Population of capital, Male: 58,000
Annual population increase: 3,8%
Religion: 100% Muslim
Language: Maldivan (Divehi), English
Currency: Maldivan Rufiyaa
Political status: Since 1965, an independent presidential republic.

KEY TO MAPS
Red: resort-hotels
Blue: atolls
Black: airport

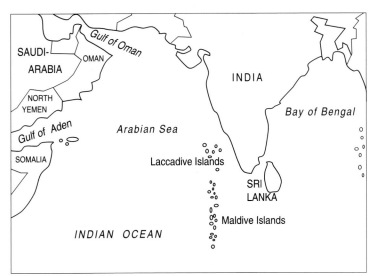